Countries Around the World

Tunisia

Marta Segal Block

Heinemann Library
Chicago, Illinois

www.capstonepub.com
Visit our website to find out more information about Heinemann-Raintree books.

To order:

☎ Phone 888-454-2279

💻 Visit www.capstonepub.com to browse our catalog and order online.

Edited by Abby Colich and Megan Cotugno
Designed by Philippa Jenkins
Original illustrations © Capstone Global Library, Ltd.
Illustrated by Oxford Designers & Illustrators
Picture research by Liz Alexander
Originated by Capstone Global Library, Ltd.
Printed in China by CTPS

15 14 13 12 11
10 9 8 7 6 5 4 3 2 1

Library of Congress Cataloging-in-Publication Data
Block, Marta Segal.
  Tunisia / Marta Segal Block.
    p. cm.—(Countries around the world)
  Includes bibliographical references and index.
  ISBN 978-1-4329-6114-5 (hb)—ISBN 978-1-4329-6140-4 (pb)
  1. Tunisia—Juvenile literature. 2. Tunisia—History—Juvenile literature. I. Title. II. Series: Countries around the world (Chicago, Ill.)
  DT245.B56 2012
  961.1—dc22   2011015497

Acknowledgments
We would like to thank the following for permission to reproduce photographs: Alamy: pp. 23 (© Clive Tully), 28 (© Harry Lands); © DrFO.Jr.Tn: p. 21; Getty Images: pp. 11 (Gamma-Keystone), 24 (Fethi Belaid/AFP), 25 (Fethi Belaid/AFP), 26 (JEBBERI/AFP), 32 (Fethi Belaid/AFP), 33 (AFP), 35 (Fethi Belaid/AFP); iStockphoto: p. 27 (© Francisco Lozano Alcobendas); Kobal Collection: p. 31 (LUCASFILM/20TH CENTURY FOX); Photolibrary: pp. 15 (URF URF), 17 (Nicolas Thibaut), 20 (Michel Gunther), 29 (FoodCollection); Photoshot: p. 18 (HELLIO VAN INGEN/NHPA); Shutterstock: pp. 5 (© WitR), 7 (© WitR), 8 (© Zvonimir Atletic), 13 (© WitR), 19 (© Agata Dorobek), 30 (© Evgeniapp), 38 (© Mishakov), 46 (© adam.golabek).

Cover photograph of Ksar Ouled Soltane, Tunisia, reproduced with permission from Photolibrary (Rene Mattes).

We would like to thank Shiera S. el-Malik for her invaluable help in the preparation of this book.

Every effort has been made to contact copyright holders of material reproduced in this book. Any omissions will be rectified in subsequent printings if notice is given to the publisher.

Disclaimer
All the Internet addresses (URLs) given in this book were valid at the time of going to press. However, due to the dynamic nature of the Internet, some addresses may have changed, or sites may have changed or ceased to exist since publication. While the author and publisher regret any inconvenience this may cause readers, no responsibility for any such changes can be accepted by either the author or the publisher.

Contents

Some words are printed in bold, **like this**. You can find out what they mean by looking in the glossary.

Introducing Tunisia

One of the smallest countries in Africa, Tunisia was until recently also one of the most peaceful. This historic peace was due to both geography and history.

Throughout most of Tunisia's history, it has more or less kept the same **borders**. These borders were not created by outside powers, but by Tunisia's geography. Tunisia is surrounded by the Atlas Mountains in the west, the Mediterranean Sea in the north and east, and the Sahara Desert in the south.

The Tunisian Republic

Tunisia's official name is the Tunisian **Republic**, or *Al Jumhuriyah at Tunisiyah* in Arabic, the official language of the country. The country is named for its capital, Tunis. Tunis is an ancient **Phoenician** city and has been the capital since the 1200s.

In December 2010, high unemployment, high food prices, and **poverty** led to street protests. In January 2011, these protests escalated and on January 14, Prime Minister Ben Ali dismissed the government and fled the country. A new "national unity" government was formed. The protests and resulting revolution are credited with sparking revolutions in other North African and Middle Eastern countries.

How to say...

Arabic is the official language of Tunisia, but many people speak a form of Arabic combined with a Tunisian **dialect**. Because Tunisia was once a **protectorate** of France, French is also widely spoken. To say *hello* in Tunisia, say *salaam aleikum*. This means "peace be to you."

Bordered on two sides by the Mediterranean Sea, Tunisia's culture has been heavily influenced by European and Arab traders.

History: A Tradition of Peace

Around 1100 BCE, **Phoenician** traders from the area now known as Lebanon began settling the Tunisian coast. The **Berber** people, both farmers and **nomads**, had already lived there for hundreds of years.

The Phoenicians came to Tunisia at the same time a **climate** change increased the size of the Sahara Desert. Travel to the area became more difficult. The city of Carthage, on the eastern side of Lake Tunis and across from the city of Tunis, was founded in 814 BCE. Carthage and Tunis broke away from the rest of the Phoenician **empire** and formed their own empire.

Romans and Vandals

In 241 BCE, Carthage lost its first war with Rome. Later Rome destroyed Carthage. The city remained deserted for 100 years. Roman control of Tunisia finally ended in 439 CE when the **Vandals**, a Germanic tribe, invaded.

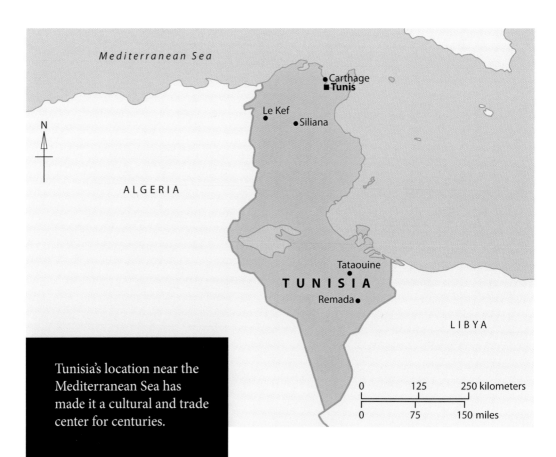

Tunisia's location near the Mediterranean Sea has made it a cultural and trade center for centuries.

Archeologists believe the remains of 20,000 children, buried between 730 and 146 BCE, are located here.

YOUNG PEOPLE

Were children sacrificed to the gods in ancient Tunisia? The ancient historian Plutarch (46–120 CE) said they were. But when Rome destroyed the city in 146 BCE, they destroyed almost all of the city's records. There is very little firsthand evidence of the culture. Between 1920 and 1970, archaeologists uncovered a cemetery filled with the remains of children, many of whom were **cremated**. Some took this discovery as proof that the ancient rumors of child sacrifice were true. Yet others believed it was simply a special cemetery for children.

The Byzantine Empire

In the 500s, Tunisia became part of the **Byzantine Empire**, a military power. From about 306 to 1453, it ruled various parts of the ancient world. It eventually fell to the **Ottoman Empire**. The Byzantine Empire was centered in Constantinople—today's Istanbul, Turkey. Constantinople's great distance from Tunis may have led to Tunisia's decline during this period. The native Berber tribes gained power, as Tunisia's cities grew smaller.

Arabs, Islam, and Berbers

In the 600s, many Arabs **converted** to **Islam** as **Muslim** armies arrived. The Berbers, often Christian, first did not convert to Islam. Over time more Berbers did convert. Today the blending of Berber and Arab-Muslim cultures has made for a unique Tunisian culture.

The Ottoman Empire

In 1574 Tunisia became part of the Ottoman Empire. It remained under Ottoman control until the 1700s. In the 1800s, Tunisia was in the uncomfortable position of being in between, geographically, the Ottoman Empire and the French. The French had invaded its western neighbor, Algeria. Tunisia came under French control in 1881.

Berber villages in the south of Tunisia are popular tourist sites. Most Tunisians have Berber heritage.

How to say...

Under the control of the Ottoman Empire, local Tunisian rulers were known as *beys*. *Bey* is a Turkish word for leader or lord. Today, the word is used as a title for men. In the 1800s, a Tunisian *bey* was the first ruler in the Muslim world to introduce a constitution to the country.

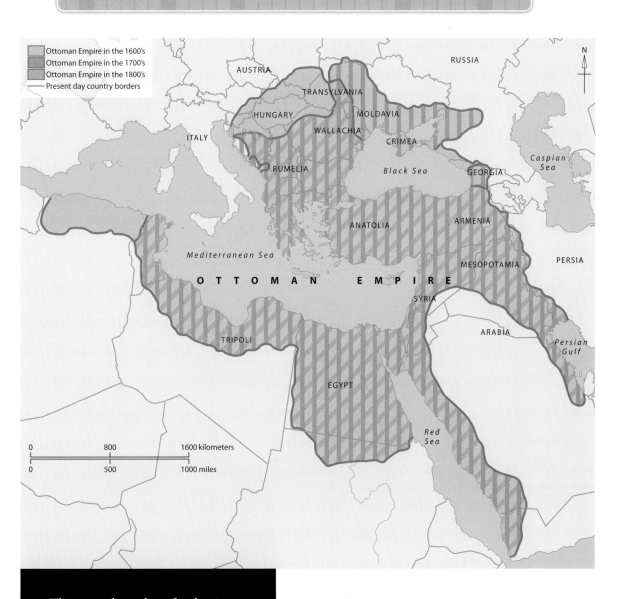

Ottoman Empire in the 1600's
Ottoman Empire in the 1700's
Ottoman Empire in the 1800's
Present day country borders

RUSSIA

AUSTRIA

TRANSYLVANIA

HUNGARY

MOLDAVIA

ITALY

WALLACHIA

CRIMEA

Caspian Sea

RUMELIA

Black Sea

GEORGIA

ANATOLIA

ARMENIA

Mediterranean Sea

MESOPOTAMIA

PERSIA

O T T O M A N   E M P I R E

SYRIA

TRIPOLI

ARABIA

Persian Gulf

EGYPT

Red Sea

0   800   1600 kilometers
0   500   1000 miles

N

This map shows how far the Ottoman Empire reached in the 1700s. The Ottoman Empire lasted from 1299 until 1923.

From protectorate to independence

Tunisia was officially a **protectorate** of France. A protectorate is a country under the economic control and military protection of another country. In contrast, many other African countries were **colonies** of European powers. Colonies have less control over themselves than protectorates do.

Few French actually lived in Tunisia, so it retained much of its own culture. The relationship continued for many years with different degrees of resistance from Tunisians. In 1942, during World War II, Germany invaded Tunisia. At the end of World War II, Tunisians were unwilling to go peacefully back to French rule. In 1956 Tunisia finally achieved independence. Tunisia's independence was much less violent than that of many other African countries.

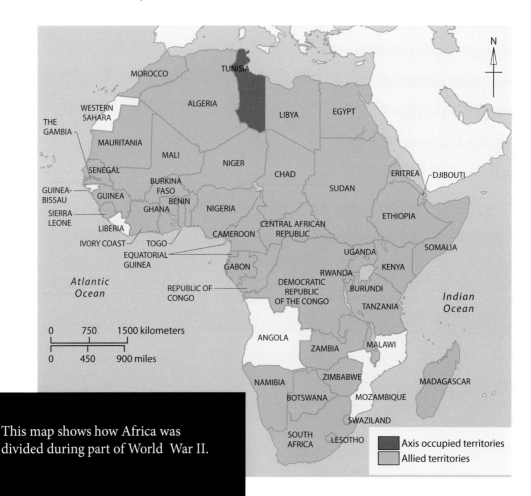

This map shows how Africa was divided during part of World War II.

HABIB BOURGUIBA (1903–2000)

Once jailed by the French for treason, Habib Bourguiba went on to become President of Tunisia for 30 years, from 1957 to 1987. Tunisia's constitution gave Bourguiba dictatorial powers, but he was generally seen as a fair ruler who responded to public opinion. Bourguiba worked to modernize the country's **economy** and social structure. A Muslim himself, Bourguiba abolished religious law and courts, and gave women more rights than they had in other Arab countries. In 1987 the elderly Bourguiba was removed from power in a bloodless takeover, or **coup**. He lived the rest of his life in his hometown, 100 miles south of Tunis.

Regions and Resources:
A Land of Contrasts

Located between the larger countries of Algeria and Libya, Tunisia is one of the smallest countries in Africa. With about 63,170 square miles (163,610 square kilometers), its area is slightly greater than the state of Georgia. Tunisia has more than 700 miles (1,100 kilometers) of coastline, connecting it to several important Mediterranean islands, including Sardinia, Corsica, Malta, and Sicily. Sicily, part of Italy, is less than 100 miles (160 kilometers) from Tunisia.

Tunisia's location has made it valuable for centuries. In the 1500s, Barbary pirates used Tunisia's coasts as a hiding place. During World War II, the coastline was considered important to both the Allies (United States, Great Britain, and France) and the Axis powers (Germany, Italy, and Japan).

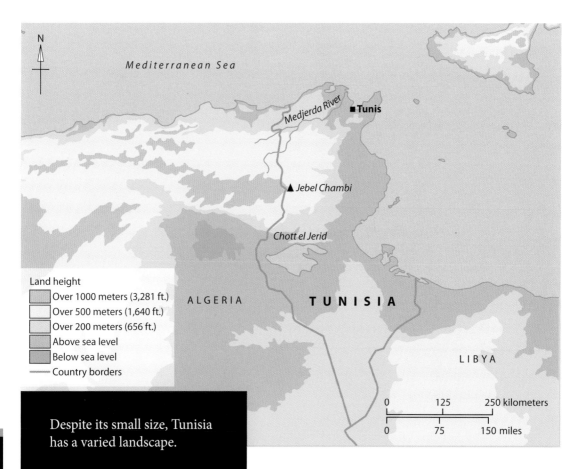

Despite its small size, Tunisia has a varied landscape.

The towns along Tunisia's Mediterranean coast look similar to other towns along the Mediterranean, such as those in Greece or Italy.

Natural resources

Before World War I, Tunisia was Europe's main supplier of **phosphates**. Phosphates are used in fertilizers, among other things. Today there is still a large phosphate and iron ore **mining** industry in the country, located mainly in the southwest and west-central areas. Tunisia is also home to a large oil industry. The country's first oil field was discovered in 1964 in the south, near Algeria. The fields benefited from a rise in **petroleum** prices in the 1970s. Today, the country's large oil reserves are partly controlled by the state-owned oil company. The natural gas industry has developed more recently.

The economy

Tunisia's wealth and resources are not spread evenly across the country. The coastal region is more developed than the inland regions. As a result, the people who live inland are more likely to be poor. However, **agriculture** plays a significant role in Tunisia's **economy**. More than one in five Tunisians work on farms or in the agricultural **sector**. Olives, grain, dairy products, beef, beets, and citrus are the country's chief agricultural products.

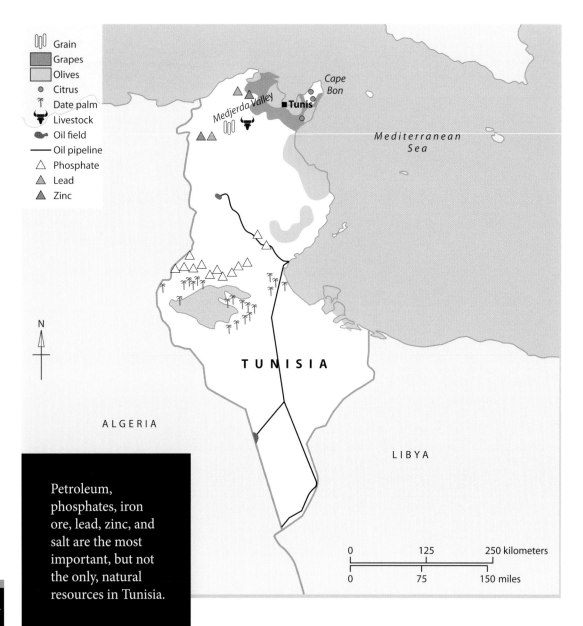

Petroleum, phosphates, iron ore, lead, zinc, and salt are the most important, but not the only, natural resources in Tunisia.

The industrial sector employs even more people—over 30 percent of the Tunisian population. In fact, there are over 10,000 manufacturing companies in Tunisia. These companies make **textiles**, shoes, and leather. Today Tunisian companies also make processed food, electronics, automotive parts, and fertilizers. The fertilizer manufacturers take advantage of Tunisia's natural phosphate reserves.

Tunisia's beaches are popular among tourists.

Textiles and tourism

Tunisia has been known for its skilled **artisans** for centuries. Their textiles have always been especially popular. Other exceptional handicrafts include jewelry, leather goods, rugs, and pottery. Today, these items are sold to tourists. Tunisia's beaches, **oases**, ancient ruins, and **mosques** are also popular with tourists.

The mountains of the north

Two mountain chains run through northern Tunisia. The Northern Tell is the lower of the two ranges. Its outline follows the coastline. Farther south, the High Tell has Tunisia's highest peak, Mount Chambi. In between the mountain chains is the Medjerda River, the only major river in Tunisia. The Medjerda River valley is known for its abundant grain and livestock.

Coastal plains

Because of its location on the Mediterranean, Tunisia's eastern coast was home to the country's most important cities. This is true today as well. The area has a typical Mediterranean **climate** with hot, dry summers and mild, wet winters. These conditions are excellent for olives and grapes—and tourism!

The Sahel

The central and inland part of Tunisia is known as the Sahel. Only 20 percent of Tunisia's area, it is home to nearly half of the country's population. The region's olive groves supplied the Romans with olive oil.

Barren areas

Central Tunisia, traditionally home to **nomadic** herders, is home to few cities even today. South of the central **plateau**, the climate becomes unbearably hot. To the far south, Tunisia gives way to the vast Sahara Desert. Parts of this region have no rainfall for years on end.

How to say...

Chott (pronounced "shott") is a French version of an Arabic word that means bank or coast. A *chott* is a salt lake in the Sahara Desert that stays dry in the summer but receives some water in the winter.

The olive groves of the Sahel have been providing Tunisia with income and olive oil for centuries.

Wildlife: Protecting the Endangered

Just as Tunisia's **climate** varies greatly, so does its animal population. Because of its location on the Mediterranean, Tunisia is along the migration path of various bird species. Storks, hawks, and eagles all make an appearance in the spring. In the fall, wading birds and waterfowl visit. Ichkeul National Park is located in the country's north. It serves as a sanctuary for water birds of all types.

The northern forests are home to many different animal species. The great variety includes wild boars, mongooses, porcupines, and genets (a catlike creature). In the south live gerbils, foxes, hares, and a kind of ground squirrel called a suslik.

The desert is filled with lizards and other reptiles including the desert varanid, a smaller relative of Indonesia's **Komodo dragon**. Horned vipers, a dangerous snake, and scorpions also live in the nearly **uninhabitable** area.

Ichkeul National Park is a well-known bird sanctuary.

In the harsh desert land, an oasis provides necessary relief.

A few desert areas are not only merely habitable, they are also pleasant. These small areas are known as **oases**. An oasis is a naturally occurring, isolated area of vegetation in the desert. The oasis typically surrounds a spring or similar water source and provides needed relief from the harsh desert. In the oasis of Tozeur, water from the natural springs is moved into ditches to water date palm groves.

The human connection

People in Tunisia have cleared woodlands to try and find more land for **agriculture**. This has caused problems for woodland animals such as the Barbary deer, nearly extinct before it was placed under protection. Other endangered species, such as the addax and the oryx (types of antelopes), ostriches, and the manned mouflon (a type of sheep), have all been reintroduced into Bou Hedma National Park.

Animals also suffer due to soil **erosion**. Natural conditions, including strong desert winds and blowing sand, make soil erosion a major problem. Humans also contribute to the problem. Poor farming techniques, such as the overgrazing of livestock, hurt the land. The government is attempting to address the problem by teaching farmers about soil **conservation**.

The Barbary Red Deer live in the wild only in Algeria and Tunisia. A group of this kind of deer has recently been introduced into Morocco.

The Medjerda River, located in Tunisia's mountainous northern region, is the only river that reliably provides water.

Humans and animals alike suffer from lack of water. The Medjerda River in the north is the only river in the country that never runs dry. The Ministry of Agriculture carefully controls all of the country's water. The ministry builds dams, drills wells, and develops **irrigation** techniques. Tunisia's water situation is made even more difficult by the toxic and hazardous waste, including **sewage**, that is not properly handled. Sewage has been known to seep into the water.

Infrastructure: A Country in Transition

In 2010 Tunisia was ranked as the 70th largest **economy** in the world. Worldwide, Tunisia ranks in the middle when it comes to personal wealth, but compared to other Arab and African countries, that ranking is quite high.

Like most countries of the world, Tunisia suffered setbacks during the worldwide financial crisis of 2009. Prior to 2009, Tunisia's peaceful history, stable government, and sound **infrastructure** helped it to attract foreign investment from countries in both Asia and Europe. While these investments have dropped off, as a whole, the country is still doing well in the 21st century.

Transportation

Since ancient times, Tunisia's strength has been in its transportation. The small country has 32 airports, 1,346 miles (2,167 kilometers) of railroad tracks, 7,863 miles (12,655 kilometers) of paved roadways, and six major seaports!

1	Saudi Arabia
2	Bahrain
3	Israel
4	United Arab Emirates
5	Qatar
6	Kuwait
7	Oman
8	Tunisia
9	Yemen
10	Jordan

The **World Bank's** Doing Business Project analyzes data to help determine which countries are best for foreign business. This list of the top Middle Eastern and North African countries shows Tunisia as a good choice for foreign companies.

For centuries, Tunisia's seaports
have welcomed trade and tourists.

A semi-democracy

Until 2011 Tunisia was technically a **republic** and with a **parliamentary government**. This means the government is organized much like those in Canada and the United Kingdom (UK). However, in practice, only one party held power in Tunisia since its independence in the 1950s.

In 1999 candidates were allowed to run against the president. Nevertheless, Ben Ali won a huge victory with almost 100 percent of the vote. Other **political parties** did, however, win some of the parliamentary seats. After the revolution of January 2011, the interim government promised to hold new elections in 2011.

Women

In 1956 Tunisia adopted the Code of Personal Status. It gave women many rights unusual for a **Muslim** country. The code outlawed **polygamy**, allowed women to request divorce, and declared that marriage must be something both people want. The role of women in Tunisia has its roots in the country's **Berber** history. In Berber tribes, women could be head of the family or head of the tribe itself.

Tunisian journalist Taoufik Ben Brik often criticizes his government. He was arrested in 2009 and sentenced to nine years in prison. In 2010 he was released. He has announced he will run for president of Tunisia in 2014.

Daily Life

In 1998 the Tunisian government set up rules that helped poor people access health care. The rules have had a positive effect. For example, in 1986, the **infant mortality rate** was 51.6 percent. Today it is 21.75 percent. In 1987 life expectancy was only 68 years. Today it is 75.9 years.

Tunisia's first president, Habig Bourguiba, supported women's rights. The country continues to support women's rights today.

Education

Tunisia is a well-educated country with a **literacy rate** of 74.3 percent. By comparison, the literacy rate in neighboring Algeria is 69.9 percent, and in Libya, it is 82.6 percent. The literacy rate in the United States is 99 percent.

Tunisian children study at the Zouhour school in Kasserine, in central Tunisia.

The Tunisian education system is based on the French school system. School is **mandatory** for all children, boys and girls, from ages six to sixteen. Students must complete thirteen years of school, while students in the U.S. must complete only twelve. The school year runs from October through June. Arabic is the main language, but starting in the second or third grade, students also learn English and French.

Daily Life

In recent years, the Tunisian government has promoted preschool education for children ages 3 to 5. There are small government-run preschools, but most children go to a *kouttab*, or Muslim preschool.

In the 700s and 800s, the Zitouna **Mosque** in Tunis was an important center of Arab learning. Today it is part of the highly regarded University of Tunis.

During the last three years of high school, students specialize in the subjects they will follow in college. Tunisia has 162 institutions of higher learning. These include colleges, technical schools, and programs for adult learners.

Culture: A Blending of Flavors

Like its culture, Tunisian food is a blend of traditions and spices. Locals enjoy native **Berber** and Arab dishes with imported European and Mediterranean spices.

Couscous, a small rice-like grain, is popular in Tunisia. It is often cooked in a *couscousiere*, a device used to steam the grain. Meat and vegetables boil in the pot's lower section, while the couscous steams on top. All is then mixed and served together. Fish and lamb are both popular in Tunisia. As in other **Muslim** countries, pork is not eaten.

Most meals are eaten with the family, but men socialize in coffeehouses with friends.

Brik (pronounced *breek*)

Brik is a popular Tunisian snack, similar to a turnover. In Tunisia the wrapping is made from a Tunisian pastry called *malsouka*. Because this snack is fried in oil, an adult must be present to help you.

Ingredients

- 1 small onion (optional)
- 1 six-ounce can of tuna
- 2 tablespoons of chopped parsley
- 2 tablespoons of grated Parmesan
- 4 eggroll or spring roll wrappers (found in most large grocery stores)
- 4 small eggs
- olive oil for frying
- lemon wedges

Method

1. Mix the tuna, parsley, Parmesan cheese, salt, and pepper.
2. Spoon about ¼ of the filling on a half of each wrapper. Make a well in the filling. Break an egg into each well.
3. Fold the wrapping into a triangle to cover the mixture and egg, and seal both sides together.
4. Fry in one-half inch of very hot olive oil. When brown, flip over to fry the other side.
5. Serve sprinkled with lemon juice.

The arts

As with Tunisia's food, its arts and literature are a spicy blend of various cultures. Tunisia's modern art often reveals influences from Roman, Ottoman, and modern European cultures.

Although Tunisia has a thriving art scene, it is best known internationally for its architecture. Like all of Tunisian culture, its architecture shows influences from Mediterranean, Arab, and African regions.

Tunisia has a very small film industry of its own, but many Hollywood movies are shot there.

During French **colonial** times, many French artists, such as Paul Klee, traveled to Tunisia to paint. In 1935 a group of Tunisian painters who had studied in Paris went back to Tunisia to found an art movement known as the Tunis school. In the language of art, a "school" is not necessarily a place where people study. It often means simply a style of painting. The Tunis school focused on recreating patterns found in traditional Tunisian **textiles**. The group also recreated stories from Tunisian folklore.

Hollywood's desert

If you are a fan of the movie *Star Wars*, Tunisia might look a little familiar to you. The film's scenes set in Tatooine (the fictional home of the fictional Luke Skywalker) were shot in Tunisia. Scenes from *The Phantom Menace* (1999), *Attack of the Clones* (2002), and *Raiders of the Lost Ark* (1981) were also filmed there. Because of Tunisia's beautiful landscapes, architecture, and advanced technology, many movies have been shot there over the years.

Festivals are a regular part of Tunisian life. Even the smallest villages hold festivals for seasonal events. The musical festivals have become well-known internationally.

Music

Tunisia's music reflects the same diverse group of influences as its other arts. *Nouba*, a very old form of music, was developed in **medieval** Spain and brought to Tunisia by immigrants in the 1500s. *Malouf* is an Arab style of music popular in Tunisia. Small groups of violins, drums, **sitars**, and flutes play this kind of music. *Bachraf* is originally from Turkey but has been part of Tunisian culture since the Ottoman period of Tunisian history. Musicians today are also heavily influenced by American jazz. Tunisia celebrates music through a wide variety of music festivals held throughout the year.

Sports

As in many African and European countries, soccer—known as football outside of the United States—is the most popular sport. The Tunisian team won the 2004 African Nations cup.

Tunisia has participated in the summer Olympic games since 1960, but the country has never participated in the winter Olympics. Tunisian athletes have won seven Olympic medals over the past 50 years. Long-distance runner Mohamed Gammoudi won four medals in the 1960s.

Mohamed Gammoudi won Tunisia's first two Olympic medals in 1964. He returned to win a gold and a bronze medal in 1968 and a silver medal in 1972.

Tunisia Today

Because of its location on the Mediterranean, Tunisia has always had a closer relationship with European countries in comparison to many other African and Arab countries. Although Tunisians certainly objected to French **colonial** rule, the rule was not as harsh as it was in other countries. This peaceful history has left Tunisia with a very good relationship with European countries today.

Fundamentalism

Like many other **Muslim** countries today, the Tunisian government and people struggle with Muslim **fundamentalists**. These groups would like the country's laws to be based on Muslim law.

An uncertain future

Following the worldwide economic collapse of 2009, many countries, including Tunisia, faced enormous financial problems. Because of its location and history, Tunisia was poised to recover quickly. However, its economic problems combined with corruption and a repressive government led to civil unrest. According to the government, 78 people were killed and 94 injured during the revolution of 2011.

New elections were held in July 2011. What will happen next is still unclear.

These students walk in Government Square in Tunis. Though life is changing for Tunisians, they hold on to many of their customs and traditions.

Fact File

Country Name:	Tunisian Republic
Capital:	Tunis
Date of Independence:	March 20, 1956
Total Area:	63,170 square miles (163, 610 square kilometers)
Climate:	temperate in northern region; desert in southern region
Highest Elevation:	Jebel ech Chambi: 5,066 feet (1,544 meters)
Lowest Elevation:	Shatt al Gharsah: 56 feet (17 meters)
Population:	10,589,025 (est. 2010)
Language:	Arabic
Religions:	Muslim (98%); Christian; Jewish
Literacy Rate:	74.3% (male: 83.4%; female: 65.3%)
Life Expectancy:	75.99 years
Median Age:	29.7 (male: 29.1; female: 30.3)
Currency:	Dinar
Agricultural Products:	olives, olive oil, grain, tomatoes, citrus, sugar, beets, dates, almonds, beef
Industries:	petroleum (gas), mining, tourism, textiles, footwear, agriculture
Exports:	clothing, textiles, agriculture products, mechanical goods, phosphates and chemicals, hydrocarbons, electrical equipment
Imports:	textiles, machinery equipment, hydrocarbons, chemicals, foodstuffs

(Source: CIA World Factbook)

National Anthem: "Humat Al Hima" ("Defenders of the Homeland")
An Egyptian wrote the first lyrics of the Tunisian anthem in the 1930s. The Tunisian national poet Aboul-Qacem Echebbi later added two more verses.

O defenders of the Homeland!
Rally around to the glory of our time!
The blood surges in our veins,
We die for the sake of our land.

Let the heavens roar with thunder
Let thunderbolts rain with fire.
Men and youth of Tunisia,
Rise up for her might and glory.
No place for traitors in Tunisia,
Only for those who defend her!
We live and die loyal to Tunisia,
A life of dignity and a death of glory.

As a nation we inherited
Arms like granite towers.
Holding aloft our proud flag flying,
We boast of it, it boasts of us,
Arms that achieve ambitions and glory,
Sure to realize our hopes,
Inflict defeat on foes,
Offer peace to friends.

When the people will to live,
Destiny must surely respond.
Oppression shall then vanish.
Fetters are certain to break.

(Source: http://www.nationalanthems.info/tn.htm)

Tunisia's UNESCO World Heritage Sites

Every year the United Nations' World Heritage Committee designates several sites as important cultural landmarks. Nine such areas are located in Tunisia:

- Roman Amphitheater of El Djem
- Archaeological site of Carthage
- Medina of Tunis
- Ichkeul National Park
- Punic Town of Kerkuane
- Medina of Sousse
- Kairouan
- Dougga (also called Thugga)

The Roman Amphitheater in El Djem is a UNESCO World Heritage site.

National Parks

Chambi: in pine forests, the park features 100 species of plants; 24 species of mammals; 16 species of reptiles; and batrachians (a kind of frog)

Ichkeul: about one hour from Tunis, the park contains 600 plant species and 200 to 300 thousand wintering water birds of 180 different species

Boukornine: vegetation forest with a great variety of animals and a great number of Persian cyclamens, a plant with beautiful flowers

Feija: cork oak forest with a rich and varied vegetation, 500 species of orchids and ferns, and 25 species of mammals, reptiles, and amphibians

Bou-Hedma: features 300 species of plants, including relics of the savanna of acacia radina (the gumtree) and many animal species such as the mouflon (small wild sheep), the ostrich, the antelope, and the gazelle

Sidi Toui: on the edge of the Sahara, this park shelters plants and wildlife typical of arid regions

The Zembra Island (and 1.5 nautical miles around the island): situated off the Gulf of Hammamet, on the edge of the Sicilian-Tunisian straits, the Zembra Park constitutes a unique island natural environment in the Mediterranean regions

National Holidays

March 20	Independence Day
April 9	Martyr's Day
May 1	Labor Day
July 25	Republic Day
August 13	Women's Day

(Many Muslim holidays are also Tunisian holidays.)

Timeline

BCE is short for Before the Common Era. B CE is added after a date and means that the date occurred before the birth of Jesus Christ, for example, 450 BCE.

CE is short for Common Era. CE is added after a date and means that the date occurred after the birth of Jesus Christ, for example, 720 CE.

BCE

1200   Phoenicians establish colony near modern-day Tunis.

814   Carthage is founded.

241   Carthage loses its war with Rome.

146   Rome destroys Carthage.

CE

439   Tunis occupied by Vandals.

622   Muhammad and followers move from Mecca to Medina.

670   Arabs move into Tunisia.

1535   Tunis captured by the French Emperor Charles V.

1574   Tunis becomes Turkish province.

1799   First agreement of friendship and trade between the United States and Tunisia.

1881   Tunisia becomes French protectorate.

1907	Young Tunisian party forms for the purpose of urging Tunisians to take control of Tunisia.
1934	Future president Habib Bourguiba becomes secretary-general of the Neo-Destour Party.
1942	German troops arrive during World War II.
1943	Germans driven out of Tunisia.
1956	Tunisia gains full independence.
1961	Tunisia becomes first Arab country to request and receive U.S. Peace Corps volunteers.
1987	Bourguiba removed from power; Ben Ali becomes president.
1999	First presidential elections with more than one party, Ben Ali still reelected.
2004	Ben Ali reelected again.
2010	In December Tunisians begin protesting against unemployment and other political issues.
2011	Protests continue, and President Ben Ali goes into exile; Prime Minister Ghannouchi resigns.

Glossary

agriculture farming; the production of crops or livestock

artisan someone skilled at making things by hand

Berber member of a group of native North African tribes

border line, either invisible or marked by a fence or boundary, that marks the difference between two countries

Byzantine Empire ruling body in various parts of the Middle East and Europe from 330 to 1453 CE

climate general weather conditions over a long time, including temperature and precipitation, such as rain or snow

colony area controlled by a foreign country; usually, people from the foreign country live in the area

conservation preservation and protection of the natural environment, including the wildlife and land

convert change someone's religious beliefs

coup (pronounced coo) takeover of a government

cremate burn a dead body until it is ashes

dialect version of a language unique to a certain area that may have different spellings, pronunciations, or words

economy management of the resources, finances, income, and expenses of a community or country

empire political unit that controls a very large area, usually broken into several separate countries or territories

erosion wearing away of something, often due to wind or water

fundamentalist someone who has a strict belief in a religion, often its ancient form and ideology

infant mortality rate measure of number of deaths of small children less than one year old

infrastructure structures such as roads, buildings, and sewers, that are necessary for a healthy society

irrigation water supplied to land for growing

Islam religious faith of Muslims, based on the Koran and teachings of the prophet Muhammad

Komodo dragon very large lizard that lives in Indonesia and that eats large animals

literacy rate percentage of people over the age of 15 who can read and write

mandatory required, sometimes by law

medieval relating to European history from about 1100 to 1453 CE

mining removing metals, rocks, or minerals from the ground

mosque Islamic religious building used for worship

Muslim follower of Islam, or having to do with a follower of Islam

nomad member of a tribe who has no permanent home, but moves from place to place

oasis (pl. oases) area of refuge in the desert

Ottoman Empire large empire, from the 1200s to the 1900s, that took over much of the area controlled by the Byzantine Empire

parliamentary government type of democracy where individuals vote for representatives, and those representatives then choose leaders

petroleum liquid in rock that can be refined to make fuel or oil

Phoenician related to an ancient country centered on the eastern side of the Mediterranean Sea

phosphate naturally occurring salt used in many chemical compounds

plateau level area of land raised above the land around it

political party organization that wants to influence the government

polygamy marriage between one man and several women

poverty being poor

protectorate country under the protection and rule of another country

republic form of government in which the people elect their leaders

sector particular part of a country's economy or society

sewage waste water and waste matter

sitar large Indian lute, or stringed instrument

textile any fabric or cloth

uninhabitable not fit or appropriate for life or living

Vandals Germanic people who invaded and destroyed parts of North Africa, among other places, in the 300s and 400s CE

World Bank international banking organization that makes loans in difficult times and helps move money among member countries

Find Out More

Books

Brown, Rosalind Varghese. *Tunisia*. Tarrytown, N.Y.: Marshall Cavendish, 2009.

Carew-Miller, Anna. *Tunisia (Major Muslim Nations)*. Broomall, Penn.: Mason Crest Publishers, 2010.

Mango Editions. *Arafat, A Child of Tunisia*. Farmington Hills, Mich.: Blackbirch Press, 2005.

Websites

www.britannica.com/EBchecked/topic/609229/Tunisia
Learn more about Tunisia from the Encyclopedia Britannica.

www.cia.gov/library/publications/the-world-factbook/geos/ts.html
The World Factbook is a publication of the Central Intelligence Agency (CIA) of the United States. It provides information on the history, people, government, economy, geography, communications, transportation, and military of Tunisia and more than 250 other countries.

www.tunisia.com
Travel guide and information in English for people who want to live, work, or visit Tunisia.

http://whc.unesco.org/en/statesparties/tn
Learn about the sites in Tunisia that the United Nations Educational, Scientific, and Cultural Organization (UNESCO) considers important to humanity.

http://tunisia.usembassy.gov/
Tunisia and the United States have a good relationship. This is the website for the U.S. embassy in Tunisia and offers information for Americans in Tunisia.

Places to visit

The Medina of Tunis

From the 1100s to 1500s, Tunis was one of the wealthiest cities in the Islamic World. The *medina*, or marketplace, was the cultural center of Tunis with schools, palaces, and mosques.

Ancient Ruins at Carthage

Founded by the Phoenicians in the 800s BCE, Carthage was destroyed and rebuilt by the Romans and later destroyed again by Muslim invaders in the 600s CE. You can see influences of all these cultures while visiting the ruins of this city.

Roman Ruins at Dougga

This ancient Roman city, believed to have been built in the 500s BCE, is one of the largest and most well-preserved ancient Roman cities in North Africa. Attractions include the city's monuments, temples, and theater.

Ksar Hadada

Visit and take a tour of the area where *Star Wars* was filmed.

Further research

Not everyone is lucky enough to visit Tunisia, but you can still find out more about this fascinating country. Pick a topic in this book that interested you, and research it further at your local library or on the Internet with the help of an adult.

Topic Tools

You can use these topic tools for your school projects. Trace the map onto a sheet of paper, using the thick black outline to guide you.

The Tunisian flag is red with a white disk in the center. In the white disk is a red crescent and red five-pointed star. The symbols reveal Tunisia's history as part of the **Ottoman Empire**. The red represents the blood shed by martyrs in various struggles; the white stands for peace; the crescent and star are symbols of **Islam**.

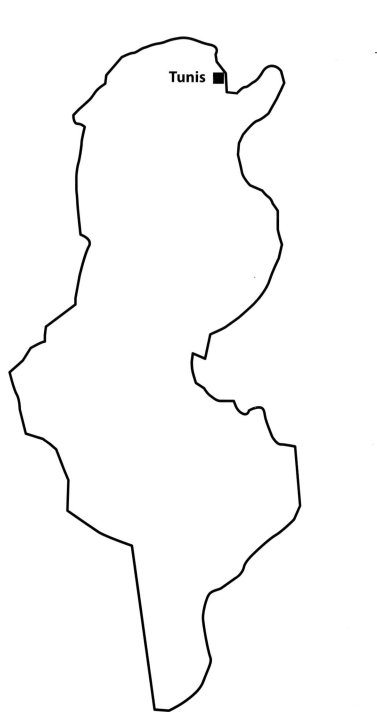

Tunis ■

N

Index

Titles in the series

Afghanistan	978 1 4329 5195 5	Japan	978 1 4329 6102 2
Algeria	978 1 4329 6093 3	Latvia	978 1 4329 5211 2
Australia	978 1 4329 6094 0	Liberia	978 1 4329 6103 9
Brazil	978 1 4329 5196 2	Libya	978 1 4329 6104 6
Canada	978 1 4329 6095 7	Lithuania	978 1 4329 5212 9
Chile	978 1 4329 5197 9	Mexico	978 1 4329 5213 6
China	978 1 4329 6096 4	Morocco	978 1 4329 6105 3
Costa Rica	978 1 4329 5198 6	New Zealand	978 1 4329 6106 0
Cuba	978 1 4329 5199 3	North Korea	978 1 4329 6107 7
Czech Republic	978 1 4329 5200 6	Pakistan	978 1 4329 5214 3
Egypt	978 1 4329 6097 1	Philippines	978 1 4329 6108 4
England	978 1 4329 5201 3	Poland	978 1 4329 5215 0
Estonia	978 1 4329 5202 0	Portugal	978 1 4329 6109 1
France	978 1 4329 5203 7	Russia	978 1 4329 6110 7
Germany	978 1 4329 5204 4	Scotland	978 1 4329 5216 7
Greece	978 1 4329 6098 8	South Africa	978 1 4329 6112 1
Haiti	978 1 4329 5205 1	South Korea	978 1 4329 6113 8
Hungary	978 1 4329 5206 8	Spain	978 1 4329 6111 4
Iceland	978 1 4329 6099 5	Tunisia	978 1 4329 6114 5
India	978 1 4329 5207 5	United States of America	978 1 4329 6115 2
Iran	978 1 4329 5208 2	Vietnam	978 1 4329 6116 9
Iraq	978 1 4329 5209 9	Wales	978 1 4329 5217 4
Ireland	978 1 4329 6100 8	Yemen	978 1 4329 5218 1
Israel	978 1 4329 6101 5		
Italy	978 1 4329 5210 5		